FOREX

Definitive Beginner's Guide

Copyright 2016- Brian StClair- All rights reserved.

This document is geared towards providing exact and reliable information in regards to the topic and issue covered. The publication is sold with the idea that the publisher is not required to render accounting, officially permitted, or otherwise, qualified services. If advice is necessary, legal or professional, a practiced individual in the profession should be ordered.

- From a Declaration of Principles which was accepted and approved equally by a Committee of the American Bar Association and a Committee of Publishers and Associations.

In no way is it legal to reproduce, duplicate, or transmit any part of this document in either electronic means or in printed format. Recording of this publication is strictly prohibited and any storage of this document is not allowed unless with written permission from the publisher. All rights reserved.

The information provided herein is stated to be truthful and consistent, in that any liability, in terms of inattention or otherwise, by any usage or abuse of any policies, processes, or directions contained within is the solitary and utter responsibility of the recipient reader. Under no circumstances will any legal responsibility or blame be held against the publisher for any reparation, damages, or monetary loss due to the information herein, either directly or indirectly.

Respective authors own all copyrights not held by the publisher.

Table of Contents

Introduction 4

Chapter 1: Forex Trading-What You Need to Know 5

Chapter 2: Finding the Right Dealer or Broker 14

Chapter 3: Basics of Analysis 22

Chapter 4: Your First Forex Trade 33

Chapter 5: Forex Beginner Trading Strategies 37

Chapter 6: Tips for Success 42

Conclusion 45

Introduction

Congratulations on purchasing *FOREX: Definitive Beginner's Guide* and thank you for doing so. There is definitely money to be made in the Forex market and purchasing this book is the first step to getting your share of it.

It is also the easiest of all of the steps, however, which is why the following chapters will help you learn everything you need to in order to trade in the Forex market successfully. You will learn what makes the Forex market unique when compared to other markets, how to find the right dealer or broker for you (and what the difference between the two is), the basic of technical and fundamental analysis and several strategies you can put to use right away. This all leads up to actually making your first trade and doing so successfully, before leaving you with a handful of tips you will want to keep in mind to ensure you find success not just in the short term but in the long term as well.

There are plenty of books on this subject on the market, thanks again for choosing this one! You will not be disappointed!

Chapter 1:
Forex Trading-What You Need to Know

Forex, commonly written as FX, is itself a shortened name for the foreign exchange currency market. Forex is the most lucrative market in the world, with more than 4 trillion dollars moving throughout it every single day. For comparison, the New York Stock Exchange does less than a tenth as much daily business. Despite its lucrative status, amateur traders were prevented from getting in on the action for decades, simply because there was no way for them to easily obtain the information required to do so successfully. Online trading has changed all of that, and now anyone with the desire to do so, and the dedication to learn everything they can about the topic, can find success just as readily as a high priced trader working for a major firm.

The first thing you need to understand about the Forex market is that it is purely speculative which means that when a Forex transaction is completed, there is nothing that is actually changing hands. Instead, the entire market, such as it is, exists as little more than numbers in a database that are then tallied to determine if your total is in the black or in the red. This is because the Forex market only came into being as a way for major corporations with offices all around the world and other global powers to take care of various expenditures without having to worry about trading currencies in the traditional sense.

Instead, they make their transactions via the forex market and everyone else speculates on how their moves are going to affect the market as a whole. In general, about 20 percent of forex transactions are made by these major entities while the rest are all investors who are hoping to make a little profit in the interim. Of this 80 percent, 80 percent are professional traders while the rest are just individuals like you.

Understanding Forex

Unlike in other markets, when a forex trader commits to a trade, they are trading a pair of currencies rather than shares of a single asset. As such, due to its very nature every forex transaction involves buying a certain amount of one currency while also selling a certain amount of a second currency. Currencies are typically trade in a few different amounts. First of all, a micro lot is 1,000 units of a currency so $1,000 is a micro lot of dollars. Next, a mini lot is 10,000 units of currency which means that $10,000 is a mini lot of dollars. Finally, a standard lot is the name given to 100,000 units of currencies which means that $100,000 is a standard lot of dollars.

Additionally, the smallest amount that a currency can move on the forex market is referred to as a pip. 1 pip equals a single percent of the total amount of the currency. When you are first getting started as a forex trader it is important to start with micro lots as when they move a pip your investment only moves 10 cents. This means that you don't necessarily need to be at the top of your game all the time at first, and builds you in some natural resistance to failure. If you purchase a mini lot then you stand to lose a dollar per every pip of negative moment and with a lot you will lose $10. Remember, currencies can often move 100 pips or more in a single day and never invest more than you can afford to lose.

While it might sound dramatically different than the more commonly seen markets available, in reality the forex market is driven by the same primary forces as the stock market, namely supply and demand. This can be seen every time the world as a whole decides that it needs more of one specific type of currency; when this occurs, prices of that currency rise. This will continue up until the point that the market once again becomes oversaturated with that type of currency and the prices starts to move back in the other direction. The best way to keep tabs on this sort of thing Is by reading reports from world powers, rumors of geopolitical strife and the current interest rate.

What further separates it from other types of investment markets is the fact that rather than reopen and close every single day, is the fact that the forex market is only ever closed from Friday night until Monday morning. While this means the market as a whole never sleeps, it doesn't mean that all of the types of currencies are traded at a single time, rather, the market is broken up into three chunks, the United States, Europe and Asia. While there is some overlap at the edges, a majority of the trading during those hours is going to be focused around pairs of currency that feature one of the currency pairs of the region in question. As an example, if you were interested in trading the US dollar then you would want to ensure you were available to do so during the American part of the day.

While there are numerous different currency pairs from all around the world, there are just 18 that are considered by most to be of the greatest importance. While this doesn't mean that you should try and trade all of the pairs at once, it does mean that you will need to be aware of them and what they are doing so you have a better forecast of the market as a whole. Even better, the 18 pairs are all from just 8 countries. While this doesn't make successful forex trading any easier, it will make it easier when it comes to knowing where to put your focus.

- *JPY* the Japanese yen
- *AUD* the Australian dollar
- *NZD* the New Zealand dollar
- *CHF* the Swiss Franc
- *GBP* the British pound
- *EUR* the euro
- *CAD* Canadian dollar
- *USD* United States dollar

Differences between forex and other markets

There are additional differences when it comes to the forex market, aside from the fact that a forex trade involves a pair of currencies that it is important to understand before your journey of forex discovery can truly be on its way. One of the most important of these is the fact that the currency market exists in an unregulated space, as opposed to the stock market's regulated status. If the market that you are trading in is regulated, then it is controlled by a centralized body or government that guarantees the results of a given trade will be as specified. These trades are then approved by various clearing houses and any disputes that arrive will be arbitrated officially by someone sanctioned by the governing body.

Instead, in the forex market, there is no centralized body to control how the market, or individual traders, behaves. This means that there is nothing guaranteeing that any of your transactions will go through as advertised because there is no one around to verify such things. Rather, each trade you make will be done through what is known as a credit agreement, the forex equivalent of a handshake. They are less binding than a traditional contract but the quid pro quo nature of the market means than you will generally have very little to worry about in terms of an individual transaction's veracity.

This ramshackle conglomeration of agreements tends to work quite well on its own because of the lack of other options should a trader decide to welch on a deal but these days most major countries also have other investor protections in place. For example, in the United States forex brokers and dealers (discussed in the next chapter) have the option of submitting themselves to the rules of the National Futures Association who handles things like arbitration if things get complicated. While not officially endorsed because there is no one to officially endorse it, this organization and others like it are especially helpful for small traders who might be afraid of losing their investment with nothing to show for it.

Additional profitable differences include things like the fact that there are no limits when it comes to short selling currency pairs so if you know a certain pair is about to bottom out then there is no reason you cannot fully take advantage of the fact. Even better, there is no such thing as insider trading in the forex market so if you know something, and you really know it, then there is nothing stopping you from fulling taking advantage of the fact. Another fun fact, there is no maximum lot size so if you had the means and the leverage to do so you could trade a billion units of currency at once and no one would bat an eye.

Finally, while forex brokers in the traditional sense can be found, they are few and far between compared to forex dealers that are much more common. The lack of brokers means that you do not need to worry about factoring in commissions when it comes to determining if you are going to make a profit. The forex market only deals in principal when means that the dealer you are working with will be looking to sell to those looking to buy and will buy from those looking to sell and then accept their own level of risk based on the current state of the market and bargain accordingly. Instead of profiting based on commissions, these individuals are looking to make money in the market in the same way that you are. These facts mean that inherently it is impossible for investors to try and buy on the bid or sell on the offer in the forex market. Instead, they have to content themselves with the fact that as soon as a trade starts making a profit, that profit goes directly into their pockets.

Currency pair basics

First and foremost, because currencies are always going to be traded in pairs, this means that one half of the pair will always be long (moving in a positive direction) while the other will be short (moving in a negative direction). To wit, if you own the pair EUR/USD and you decided to sell a standard lot then what you are doing is basically trading the euros that you own and trading them for US dollars which you expect to soon be worth more than you paid for them. As such, you decided to go short on EUR and long on USD.

The currency pairs that you are going to need to get to know include the following:

- EUR/USD – euro – US dollar
- USD/JPY – US dollar – Japanese yen
- USD/JPY – US dollar – Japanese yen
- GBP/USD – British pound – US dollar
- USD/CHF – US dollar – Swiss franc
- EUR/JPY – euro – Japanese yen
- GBP/JPY – British pound – Japanese yen
- EUR/GBP – euro – British Pound

Aside from these, there are three additional pairs that are known as the commodity pairs because their currencies are closely tied to various commodities that they produce. Combined with those above they account for more than 90 percent of all of the transactions that take place in the forex market in a given day. The commodities pairs are:

- AUD/USD – Australian dollar – US dollar
- USD/CAD – US dollar – Canadian dollar
- NZD/USD – New Zealand dollar – US dollar

When trading in the forex market, you will find that currency quotes are handled in a very precise fashion. First of all, the currency that comes first in the pair is considered the base currency and the other is referred to as the quote currency.

Furthermore, you will find that most quote are written in dollars as in $1 per amount of the currency in question, even if USD is not in the pair being traded.

Additionally, each quote will contain a bid price and also what is known as an ask price. The bid price is the amount that a forex dealer will be able to purchase the pair for while the ask price is what the short currency can be sold for in exchange for the long currency. The difference between the bid and the ask is referred to as the spread.

Other facts to consider

Leverage: When it comes to forex, you can consider leverage money that you can borrow to hopefully see a greater return on a currency pair that you know is going to increase in value substantially. This money can be obtained from a broker or a dealer and rates as high as 100:1 can be found in some places online. If taken advantage of, it means that for $100 you can basically control 10,000 currency units instead. Leverage goes both ways, however, so you could just as easily be out 10,000 credit units as you could be up 10,000 credit units.

A note on margin: When you start actively trading in the forex market, you are going to need to keep in mind that the concept of margin works differently in the forex market as opposed to other markets. As such, in the forex market you will find that margin cannot accurately be thought of as a way to place a down payment of an equity that you want to purchase in the future. Rather, it should consider a deposit into your account that will be used to protect you from losses in the future. As a general rule, the greater the amount of leverage you can obtain on a deal, the greater the margin well be.

Furthermore, you will want to remember that return is always going to be driven by yield so essentially you are always selling one currency in order to purchase another currency instead. You will also need to keep in mind that you will have to always pay for the interest on the currencies you are selling, but they will generally be canceled out by the currencies you are purchasing.

Rollover: Another rule when it comes to the forex market is that all trades have to be finished in just 48 hours. There is a safeguard in place if this cannot happen, however, and it is what is known as rollover. A rollover will allow you an extra two days to make a specific trade in return for an extra chunk of interest. You can utilize a rollover if you need more time with a given trade, or you can trade in rollovers exclusively as part of the forex market. In a rollover the difference between the starter interest amount and the new interest amount is typically visualized via something called an overnight loan. When this occurs the trader in need of extra time holds onto a long positon connect to a higher interest rate currency to initiate the rollover. The amount related to two different rollovers is never going to be the same and the specifics for a given rollover can change over a period of days, or even hours.

Chapter 2:
Finding the Right Dealer or Broker

The fact that the forex market is open 24 hours a day 5 days a week, and more than 4 trillion worth of transactions move through it each day means that there are always going to be new brokers or dealers coming onto the scene in hopes of making a profit somewhere along the line. As such, if you ever hope to have any real success in the forex market, the first thing you are going to need to do is separate the wheat from the chaff and find the broker or dealer that actually suits your needs.

While one might hope the process of finding a dealer or broker that is honest and easy to work with would be as simple as finding any other type of review online, unfortunately that is not the case. This is because two different companies might phrase the same costs and benefits in very different ways, and many forex dealers will actually call themselves brokers, simply because this is a word that more people are already familiar with. Luckily there are a few things you can always do to ensure you are getting off on the right foot.

1. *Understand what separates brokers from dealers:* The first thing you are going to want to do when looking for a company to work with when it comes to actually making trades is determine if you are dealing with an actual broker, a dealer in broker's clothing or just an honest dealer. For starters, you are going to be able to easily determine if you are working with a dealer instead of a broker if they are willing to take trades themselves, instead of simply setting them up for the clients that they see.

On the other hand, you will be able to determine if a broker is a real broker and not a dealer in broker's clothing if they are not able to actually trade with you and instead set you up another one of their clients who wants the opposite side of the same trade. To clarify, it might help if you think about brokers as though they are real estate agents and the currency pairs up for trade are the properties for sale. Meanwhile, dealers can be more accurately thought of as property wholesalers, taking profitable trades when they find them and passing them along for a profit.

2. *Know the level of regulation:* When looking for the dealer or broker that most accurately meets your needs, you are always going to want to take in to consideration the amount of regulation that they are operating under, not just what their rates and promises are. Simply put, the greater degree of regulation they are subject too, the less likely you have to worry about them walking away with your money. This is a not insubstantial concern when working with online brokers or dealers which is why you need to always speak with a real person and ask to see proof that they are regulated in the way they appear to be.

This is why it is best to deal with a dealer or broker who lives in your part of the world, so that you know you will have the easiest time tracking down help if it is required. Remember, if you choose to go with a dealer who is located in a far off land with no regulation, you have no regulation at the market level to fall back on which means you could be out your investment and the victim of fraud well before you even realize it. These are not issues you want to have to worry about while still learning the ins and outs of forex trading, do yourself a favor and find as much regulation as possible.

Additionally, you are going to want to consider the finances of the dealer or broker you are working with, especially if they are not as regulated as they should be. Without the right sort of regulation, it is entirely possible that if the market turns in a certain direction your dealer will find themselves belly up, which in turn means that you are out your deposit, with no one to turn to for restitution. Don't be drawn in by promises of wide spreads, stick with a regulated, financially stable dealer, it really is the best choice.

3. *Be aware of capitalization concerns:* Outside of ensuring that your dealer or broker is regulated, you will also want to know what amount of capital that they are working with. While brick and mortar institutions are likely not going to have to close up shop after a bad week, you never know what an online dealer is working with unless you ask. Additionally, you will want to visit the Commodity Futures Trading Commission website at CFTC.gov as it shows the current amount of capitalization that all of its members are currently working with. If you are looking for brokers or dealers outside of the United States, checking with a local regulatory body for this type of information is typically the best place to start.

4. *Know what platforms they support:* If you are completely new to all types of trading them you won't have any trading platform preferences that you will need to take into account when it comes to choosing a dealer or broker to work with. If you are already committed to a specific platform, however, then you are

going to want to ensure that the dealer or broker that you are working with is compatible as well.

If you haven't chosen a trading platform yet then you are going to want to seek out MetaTrader 4, it is free and widely considered the best trading platform on the market as of 2016. MetaTrader 4 currently holds 85 percent of the entire market and comes with plenty of features that you won't be able to appreciate properly for quite some time. The MetaTrader platform is available at MetaTrader.com and the site provides a great overview of various features and explanations of whether or not it is the right platform for you.

5. *Factor in the costs:* If you end up working with a dealer then you are going to be working with a fee structure that is set by someone known as the market maker. The market maker is the person who you can count on to buy when you want to sell, and sell when you want to buy. To factor in how much a given dealer is going to charge you, you care going to want to consider the number of pips in the spread between what buyers are paying and what sellers are receiving. The bigger the spread, the more that dealer is going to end up costing you in the long run.

If, however, you instead try and seek out an actually forex broker then you will be making trades with the help of what is known as the Electronic Communications Network in order to make trades. This network is used by all forex brokers and it connects buyers and sellers all around the world. Because brokers in these cases aren't actively buying or selling against their clients they make their money based on a commission that you would pay per transaction. This, in turn, means their spread will be tighter overall which means they are more useful in some situations and less useful in others.

To illustrate, consider the following example, say you come across a currency pair, AUD/USD, and you are confident that it is going to only increase in value in the short term. This means you are going to want to investigate a long position; if you are using a dealer then you might discover that the pair is available with a 5 pip spread. If you take this deal, then you are going to need for AUD to move in the right direction a total of 6 pips before you stand to make any profit. Assuming you are trading a mini lot then each pip is worth $1 and it would cost you $50 to set up, however, once AUD moved 6 pips in the right direction, everything after that is nothing but profit.

Alternatively, if you instead decide to approach this same transaction with the help of a broker then you might find yourself on the Electronic Communications Network looking at a 1.5 pip spread instead. In this case each trade that you made would cost you a blanket $2.50, in addition to the spread and other commission costs which means that you will be making more money on bigger trades while making less on smaller trades.

Finally, you are going to need to determine the amount of leverage that each potential dealer or broker is currently offering. In the United States, the maximum allowable leverage is 50 to 1. However, if you go outside of the country for your dealer needs you can easily find leverage of as much as 700 to 1 in some instances. In these cases, you will need to take into account the margins that each potential dealer or broker is working under as well.

6. *Compare available services:* When looking for the right type of broker or dealer for you, it is important to make sure that you take the time to shop around for long enough that you get a sense of the various amenities and services being offered currently. You will also want to determine what types of accounts they have that are currently available (options typically include demo accounts, micro accounts, mini accounts and standard accounts) the biggest difference between them is the size of the largest trade that the account is cleared ahead of time to make. The amount that is connected to each will likely vary between individual brokers and dealers, another reason why it will pay for you to ask around and determine what a fair going rate currently is.

Outside of trade limits, the most notable difference that you are likely to come across when comparing various dealers and brokers is going to be the spread that you are going to have to abide by as well as any applicable commissions that are going to be charged. This number is also likely to vary between various options, as well as based on the overall strength of the market, user forums are often a good place to go if you are interested in the quality of the spread over a prolonged period of time. Brokers are also likely to through in extra services as a way of justifying their commission, if you are interested in going this route, it is important to speak with a person at the brokerage and ask about additional benefits.

While additional perks are nice, one of the most important facets of any good broker or dealer is their customer service experience. This means that while doing research you are going to want to pay close attention to how hard you have to look to find a way to speak with a real person as this is likely an indication of home difficult it is going to be for you to find satisfaction if a call to their customer service center is required. As a new forex trader, if you have a problem you are going to want to ensure that you have some ready to help you handle it as quickly as possible, not after you are given the runaround and forced to deal with countless unhelpful phone menus. To prevent this, ensure that the broker or dealer you choose can be contacted in at least two functional ways and for at least 12 hours each day. This might seem like a hassle up front, but safe is most certainly better than sorry when your investments are at stake.

Finally, it is important to always keep in mind that your business is an important commodity to any online broker or dealer these days because the competition in the field is so extremely fierce. As such, it is not uncommon for brokers or dealers to throw in extras in hopes of out-valuing their competition. This means you are always going to want to ask about additional services or products that come with the account, especially because as a new trader there is a greater chance that you can use them. Don't underestimate the value of free classes, extra analysis or improved signals, especially if they are free.

7. *Ask the right questions:* After you have narrowed down your search to the best possible dealers and brokers, the last thing you are going to want to do is speak with a

representative from each of the companies in question and ask them numerous questions just to make sure that everyone is on the same page. Some of the questions you are already going to want to be familiar with, but it is important to understand how they are answered as much as it is to know the answer at face value.

It is important to know what countries they are currently regulated in as well as the currency pairs that they offer for trade. You will want to know if the customer deposits are separated from any operating capital, what trading platforms they support and if they utilize the Electronic Communications Network and if there are any limits placed on account types. Finally, you will want to ask about customer service and the process for depositing or withdrawing money.

Chapter 3:
Basics of Analysis

After you have gone ahead and picked a dealer or broker to start working with on a regular basis, as well as a platform that works for you, the next thing you are going to need to learn about is how to look at a given forex trade in the right light thanks to proper analysis. There are two primary types of analysis, technical and fundamental, and while fundamental is the more common these days, technical analysis is experiencing somewhat of a renaissance. The biggest difference between the two is their opinion on information outside of what the price of a currency currently is.

Fundamental analysis believes in looking at the big picture to determine if a currency is worth more than the market currently says while technical analysis focuses only on the price as it currently stands. Due to this divide, fundamental analysis will always take longer to perform than technical analysis simply because sometimes you have to wait for new financial information to be available before you have anything to actually act upon. It is also easier to use and requires less training in order to use properly, however, so it is still the preferred choice in most instances.

Fundamental Analysis

Fundamental analysis is at its most useful when it is being used to gather a broad idea of what the market is likely to do in the near future from numerous variables as well as changes that occur in monetary policy in various countries throughout the world. The ultimate goal here is to find the currency pairs that are currently valued below what fundamental factors predict and purchase them before the price catches up with the facts. There are numerous steps to performing fundamental analysis and they are outlined below.

1. *Find the baseline:* When it comes to analyzing the fundamentals of specific currency pairs, you are going to need to start by establishing a baseline in terms of worldwide economics and the prices of various currencies so that you have a good idea of when things actually start to change. To determine a baseline, you are going to want to start by considering relevant global macroeconomics to ensure you gather the right type of data that is actively affecting the currencies in question. You will also want to consider the way that the currencies have behaved in the past as previous behavior is often a solid indicator of the future as well.

   Additionally, when it comes to gathering past data you are going to want to determine the current phase that the currency is in. Each currency has three phases, if the related currency is booming then liquidity will be high and volatility will be low; if it is in a bust period then liquidity will be low and volatility will be high. Additionally, currencies can be in a pre or post bust phase as well as a pre or post boom phase. Accurately picking out the current phase of the currency is a key to becoming a successful forex trader and finding profit where others miss out on the profits that you found easily.

To determine where a currency is currently at, in terms of its overall level of quality, you are going to want to start by checking the default rates as well as reserve accumulation levels and bank loan rates. As a general rule, lower numbers are an indicator of a stronger market, but if the market has been strong for too long, then you know a bust is likely on the way and will need to plan accordingly. The market is often slow to react to these types of things which means that taking advantage of them early and often can lead to big payouts in the sooner than later.

2. *Think about global factors:* After you have a solid idea of what the current economic phase is looking like, you will then want to start considering possibilities that would result in economic expansion when it comes to the currency or currency pairs you are surveying. In order for this step to be effective, you are going to need to do more than simply look for obvious signals, you are going to need to dig deep if you hope to find anything useful before the market has adjusted to account for it. A good place to look for this sort of thing is in the tech industry where emerging technology can quickly turn an entire economy around in a major way.

These types of indicators are often useful when it comes to pointing out a boom phase that is likely to last as long as it takes for the technology to fully integrate into the mainstream at which point it becomes a going concern and not something new. This point is likely also going to be the start of a bust period which means you are going to need to be cautious if you still plan to make money in the speculative market during this period. Likewise, you are going to want to prioritize leverage points that are smaller than you might otherwise be interested in while also minimizing long term position until things start to balance out. On the other hand, if you find yourself just entering a boom phase then you can safely increase your minimum allotted risk, at least until things turn back the other way.

3. *Think globally:* In addition to the current economic forecast of the region whose currency you are interested in trading, you will also want to take a broader look at what things are like worldwide. To do this you are going to simply want to apply the same analysis to the worldwide economy that you did to the individual economy, starting with major interest rates. This means you are going to want to look at the European Central Bank, the Federal Reserve, the Bank of Japan, the Bank of England, etc. You will also need to take into account various biases when it comes to policy and what their legal mandates look like. This will help you to have a better idea of which regions are currently seeing the greatest amount of supply growth when it comes to money as well as what is currently going on when it comes to emerging markets, market volatility and future interest rate expectations.

4. *Look to the past:* After you have a clear idea of the current state of worldwide fiscal policies as well as those in the countries you are most interested in, you will then be able to compare current events to the events of the past in an effort to determine the true state of things as they stand in the moment. Not only will this give you an overall idea of the current relative level of strength of your country of choice's economy, it

will give you an idea of how long you might be able to expect the current phase to last if you do decide it is the right time to invest. Remember, if you are looking to make easy money, then the period directly after a bust is the time to do so as long as traditional credit channels have not been completely exhausted. At this point you can have the maximum amount of allowable risk that will then immediately start to decrease up until the point things flip back in the other direction.

5. *Look into volatility:* It is important to understand how volatile the market currently is before committing to any forex trade and the best and most reliable way to do so is by simply looking to the stock market for the answers. The more stable the stock market is, the more secure people feel with their current investment choices and the more stable the forex market remains as a result. It is important to keep in mind that the stock market can vary greatly, no matter what phase the economy is in or how long it has been there which means you will always want to hope for the best while at the same time still planning for the worst. In this case the more robust the boom phase is, the lower the overall level of volatility is going to be while the opposite is also going to be true.

6. *Choose the right pairs of currency:* After you have a good idea of what you can expect from the market overall, the next thing you are going to want to do is to actually find the pairs of currency that you plan on selling. This can be accomplished by first looking at all the currency pairs based on the currencies you are most familiar with and then find the point where the gap between the two is the biggest as far as their interest rates go. You will also need to know what each of the

pair is currently up to and thus, how likely they are to remain in the current position.

To determine these specifics, you are going to want to start by determining the difference between the countries' output gap and their current rate of unemployment. When looking at these numbers you are going to want to keep in mind that as constraints to capacity increase and unemployment drops then shortage will set in and lead the economy to a state of inflation. This will then lead interest rates to rise in response, which will ultimately result in a cooling of the economy. Taking the time to keep an eye on this situation will ultimately make it easier for you to determine how the currency pair interest rate disparity is going to look in the near future.

What's more, you will also need to keep in mind various balances when it comes to payments between nations that involve either of the currencies in question. Remember, the healthier a given country's debt and capital ratio is, the stronger any currencies related to that country are going to be, even if disaster strikes. To find this number you will need to find the amount of capital that each country is currently working with as well as the overall position of both nations in terms of things like foreign investment and accumulation of reserves.

7. *Consider relative trade strength:* If a country is currently in a phase of growth, the stronger its currency fundamentals remain, the greater the likelihood that those who are currently holding onto it are going to continue to do so. This will also be the case if the currency in question has a relatively high overall

interest rate when compared to similar currencies. This means that during the early parts of a boom phase you will find a strong market for various types of currencies that combine agreeable interest rates with strong fundamentals. Likewise, if you can find higher interest rates then you can manage to overlook fundamentals that are rather subpar.

Technical Analysis

Technical Analysis is all about the belief that the way that the price of a currency has acted in the past is always going to be the most reliable way to predict how it is going to act in the future. As the forex market is almost always on the move, if you follow technical analysis it means that you never are going to be at a loss for data. With this in mind you can then pick a pair of currencies to track and then use numerous different technical tools, such as trends, indicators or charts to find out where things are likely to go next. While it can get quite complicated at times, technical analysis is really just the study of supply and demand with the hope of finding a profitable trend along the way.

Technical analysis is about more than just a means to determine the intrinsic value a currency currently holds, it is a tool for finding patterns that can affect the entire market and acting on them in a quick enough fashion that you can make a profit in the process. In order to work properly, technical analysis holds three things to always be true. First, prices are always going to move the way that trends predict. Second, the market will ultimately discount everything. Third, history is always going to repeat itself, it just might take its time in doing so.

- *The market will eventually discount everything:* While those who haven't yet seen the light may think that technical analysts only focus on the price of a given currency and nothing else, the truth is that they only focus on the currency price because they believe that the market has already taken everything else into account beforehand. As such, there is no need to look at anything else as the current price is a reflection of everything else that has happened up to this point. This, in turn, makes it the most accurate judgement of price possible, bar none.

- *Prices move based on trends:* After you have determined an apparent trend when it comes to the past performance of a given currency then technical analysis states that you are much more likely to be able to relate it to similar trends that will develop in the future. The most effective technical strategies for trading always assume that future trends are predicated on those that have come before.

- *History is always going to repeat itself:* If technical analysis moves based on trends, then logic would state that currency prices are going to repeat themselves eventually as well. Technical analysis believes that those who interact with the market are prone to the same type of responses when the market responds in certain ways. With this in mind it then becomes easy to put together data regarding past trends and then watch for the market to respond in the way it has in the past as people react in the same ways time after time after time. This reaction can then also be plotted using existing patterns as a way of accurately determining which trends are going to start at what point and how you can expect to best capitalize on them.

All about trend

In order to get the most out of technical analysis you are also going to need to understand how trend work and the effect it has on analyzation. For starters, a trend is any noticeable assemblage of price data pointing in either a positive or a negative direction that indicates what direction the market is likely to move in the near future. Trends can either be obvious as well as strong or weak and mostly obscured. This means that you will always need to be on the lookout for potential trends, while at the same time not reading too much into market noise that you end up going in the wrong direction.

This can be quite a difficult task sometimes, as prices can often be known to move around erratically, or clump together in an ultimately meaningless fashion. This means that in order to get a clear picture of what exactly is going on you will need to just look for an overall pattern in terms of the highest highs or the lowest lows. This means that it doesn't matter if every price point confirms to a pattern as long as a majority do in one way or the other.

Positive trends are referred to as uptrends and negative trends are referred to as reversals. Additionally, there are horizontal trends when the lows and the highs essentially balance one another out. What's more, you are also going to want to be on the lookout for the length of the various trends that you discover as a trend can either be long term or short term depending on its overall length. If you discover a short trend you are going to want to go ahead and look at all of the available information because a short trend might really just be a facet of an overall longer and more prevalent trend. An easy way to determine what exactly it is that you are looking at is to ensure you are always considering charts that cover multiple time spans as charts covering longer spans can make it easier for you to see the forest for the trees when it comes to understanding what exactly is going on.

After you have found a trend that you are interested in pursuing, the next thing you are going to want to do is to add in a trendline to make it clear exactly what it is you are looking at. If the trend that you find is following an uptrend, then you will want to connect the dots of the lowest points of the trendline so that the line is underneath the relevant data. If the trend that you uncover is a downtrend, then you are instead going to want to connect the highest points so that the trendline is above the data in question. If the line is above the data then it is said to represent the market's resistance to a price increase and if it is below the data the it is said to represent the support that the market is giving off to keep the price at a specific point if not higher. This line is not useful when it comes to determining the overall likelihood that a trend will continue, just what the likely movement is going to be if it does.

Additionally, channel lines are two lines that can be drawn on either side of the data to indicate both support and resistance. One of these lines will connect the various high points while the other will connect all of the low points. The channel that is created by connecting those dots can then itself either move up, down or horizontally but it will clearly be one of the three regardless. When performing this exercise, you are going to want to ensure that the channel you create is long enough that it will eventually note the point where the data breaks through the channel. This is the point that you are going to want to take advantage of as the breaking point indicates that a substantial amount of movement is on the horizon.

Chapter 4:
Your First Forex Trade

Once you are ready and able to make your initial foray into forex trading, it is important that you approach it with the idea that, no matter how adept at trading you become, you will never reach a point where all of your trades are going to be an automatic success. Where you are going to improve, however, in in your ability to accurately anticipate the way the price of a currency is going to move, your ability to manage risk and your ability to analyze the market correctly on the fly. Then, over time, you will find that while you do not have the ability to predict every trade correctly, you will have the ability to make a reliable profit simply because you make the right trade more often, and more reliably, than you make the wrong one all of the time. This then, is the true market of a successful forex trader.

Create your own forex trading plan

When it comes to interacting with the forex market, it is important that you never do so without having a plan in place first. To create your own successful forex trading plan, you are going to want to start by deciding on which currencies you are particularly interested in as well as how long you plan on holding individual pairs for before trading them off again. With the general specifics out of the way, you are then going to want to determine how much you have to start investing in the forex market with, how much time you plan to spend trading in the forex market each week and what you hope to see as a return on your investment in both the short as well as the long term.

With this in mind, you will then be able to determine how much you can realistically make in a given period of time. If you like the calculations you come up with, then great, otherwise you are going to need to either change the amount of trading you are going to do on a regular basis or alter the amount of risk you are willing to take on an individual trade. What you must never do, however, is set daily trading goals for yourself. Setting daily goals will only encourage you to take unnecessary risks at the end of each trading day, which will either cost you money in the long run or teach you that bad trading habits are acceptable, which will ultimately cost you more money in the long run. If you feel the need to set goals for yourself, make them monthly goals instead.

Don't forget to think about how you are going to find currency pairs to trade as well as the criteria that you will base all good trades on. Knowing these specifics will help you to properly mitigate risk via automated stop loses and make you more successful overall. After you have all the details in place for your plan, it is extremely important that you stick with it no matter what. This doesn't mean choosing to stick with it at the start of each trading session when you are fully in control of your emotions, it means making a commitment and sticking with it even when you are extremely tempted to let your emotions take over and make a specific choice only as a means of getting back at the market.

Finally, it is important to keep track of your results so that you have an idea of how effective your plan actually is. While you won't want to analyze your daily results, you will want to analyze your results at the end of a set period of time, this means you are going to want to track every single trade, the date and time it was made, which currency pair it included, the price for each half of the pair and the end results. If after two weeks you don't have a 60 percent trade average or better, you will want to take another look at your plan.

Making a trade

The following is a walkthrough of how to make a forex trade, it should be largely accurate regardless of what trading platform you are currently using.

1. Make sure you have chosen a broker or dealer that is compatible with your platform of choice.

2. Start by selecting a currency pair you are interested in and that you have been researching. For this example, you will be trading the euro and the US dollar so EUR/USD.

3. Next you will be taken to a screen which shows you the specific details on the pair in question. This will include the price for both halves of the pair as well as what the broker or dealer is currently offering in terms of the spread.

    In the EUR/USD example above, the details can be written thusly:

    Long Currency EUR

    Short Currency USD

    Buy Price 1.3080

    Sell Price 1.3040

4. With an idea of what prices are currently like, you will then want to use various strategies, including those

discussed in detail in the next chapter, to decide if you want to move forward with the trade in question.

5. *Find your position:* With your mind full of the required research, you are then going to want to move forward with a speculative position. It is important to keep in mind that you have the ability to make money on the forex market no matter what direction it moves in as long as you speculate properly. When you make the decision to purchase a specific currency, what you are really doing is expressing a belief that the long currency is going to increase in value and the short currency is going to decrease in value. In the example above, for instance you would be indicating that you believe the euro will soon be acting in a bullish fashion while the US dollar is going to soon be acting bearish.

Chapter 5:
Forex Beginner Trading Strategies

Long Term Strategy

When you are just starting out in trading in the forex market, one of the types of strategies you are likely going to use the most is what is known as a carry trade. In this type of strategy, you are going to find a currency pair that you expect to move in a profitable direction, that also has an extreme disparity between the interest rates of the currency in question. These types of currency pairs are generally going to include either the New Zealand dollar, the Japanese yen or the Australian dollar. A common scenario you will find is that the Australian or the New Zealand dollar will often have an interest rate of as much as 4.5 while at the same time the Japanese yen will be sitting somewhere close to .1. When this is the case you will want to purchase AUD/JPY.

What makes carry trades so great is that they will generate a profit for you via their interest every single day that you hold onto them. What's more, this payout will be paid every day that the market is open with weekend payments coming on Wednesdays. This means that you will always want to wait until Thursday to close out carry trades. To find out how much you will be bringing in each day from the interest rate disparity, the first thing you are going to want to do is subtract the short currency interest rate from the long currency interest rate. Next you will multiply that answer by the number of units that you are currently holding that relates to the interest rate in question, including leverage. Finally, you will divide the result by 365 to find your daily profit margin. The carry trade is a great choice or traders who don't want to spend every moment looking at a computer screen.

The carry trade gained popularity in the early 00s when AUD/JPY often had a difference in interest rates of over 5 percent. While this on its own wouldn't have catapulted it into the spotlight, during this same period leverage was regularly being offered at rates of 200:1. Combined, these factors lead to millions of dollars being gained and lost every day as many people jumped in without fully learning how to utilize them properly.

Proper utilization: You will know it is time to use a carry trade when your research reveals that the central bank related to a favor currency pair either has, or is soon going to, raise its interest rates. This information will then be followed by many people jumping into the carry trade, making the difference even greater and more profitable. The fact that there is going to be a run on the currency pair in question means that you need to be aware of the incoming change as quickly as possible so that you can take advantage of it to the fullest.

Limited application: While carry trades can be extremely profitable in certain situations, when using them it is important that you understand that they are not always going to be the right choice every time. For example, when you find out that a country with a high interest rate is going to cut it, then you should know that everyone who is currently using it as part of a carry trade is going to bail, dropping the difference between the two even more. A similar response is also likely to come about after average annual yield drops while exchange rate variance increases. You will also need to be aware of any plans that a central bank might have when it comes to forcibly changing the direction a currency is currently moving in.

Basket carry trade: If you have a clear indicator as to the direction he market is likely going to head then a standard carry trade is likely going to work just fine. On the other hand, if the indicator isn't as clear as you might like, then you will likely want to go with what is known as a basket carry trade instead. In a basket carry trade instead of purchasing a single pair, you are going to want to purchase three different pairs that have different levels of disparity when it comes to their interest rates. This way, regardless of the direction that the market moves in, you can be sure that you are going to make a profit one of the three, make a smaller profit on the second and the third will expire unprofitable.

Short Term Strategy

When it comes to trading forex in the short term, it is important to be able to exercise supreme control when it comes to both sticking with a plan or managing risk as effectively as possible. Doing so will allow you to generate as much control as possible, while still working with charts that deal in shorter overall time frames. That doesn't mean you will only need to focus on the short term charts to trade in the short term successfully, on the contrary, this is definitely a recipe for disaster.

First and foremost, you are going to want to find two different moving averages based on an hourly chart. The platform that you are using should automatically be able to generate these based on the time frame that you provide. You will then be able to use the indicators that are generated as a sort of guidepost for the strategy in question, making it easier for you to see what is likely to be happening in a slightly longer term time frame. If the short moving average that you have found is lower than the larger moving average then you are going to want to consider going long, and going long hard.

After this trend has been properly determined and you have found a bias to work with you will then want to consider entries that match the direction of the trend in question. Your goal here to is to find the momentum that you have found on the longer charts back on the shorter 5 or 15 minute charts that you started off in.

During this strategy it is important to keep in mind that just because you are looking to buy, doesn't mean the timing is always going to be right for you to do so. Instead, you will need to wait for a profitable position to trigger which means you will need to find an exponential moving average. The trigger in question is going to be an 8 period exponential, built on a 5-minute short term chart. You will know that it is time to buy when you see the price cross this 8 period exponential on the 5-minute chart, moving in the direction of the overall trend. This means the trend is soon going to be back with a vengeance and buying will be a profitable choice.

Benefits: When it comes to benefits, the biggest one in this strategy is that waiting for the trigger means there will always be other short term traders creating action for the pair in question which means there is always money for savvy traders to make. Additionally, this is a great choice for those who don't have much to start with in terms of investment capital because, when used correctly, it will let trader pick up certain currencies early before momentum has moved in a bullish direction. Alternatively, it will let traders get rid of currencies for a maximum value as well, as they can get in before the benefits of momentum moving in the other direction instead. When using this strategy, you will want to keep in mind that when a price goes through a short term retracement it is going to cause the price to swing.

As such, you are going to want to place your stop losses just below the previous high water mark to prevent yourself from losing out on an otherwise great deal. On the other hand, if you are working with short positions then you are going to want to find stops that are higher than the previous low point so that you don't lose out if things don't continue moving in the direction you were hoping for. The flexibility that can be seen in this strategy is perhaps its greatest strength, as long as you have the emotional fortitude to set your stops early and use them liberally instead of staying in just a little longer in hopes of recouping unrelated losses.

Risks: It is important to keep in mind that working with short terms can be very risky, simply because things can change dramatically in an exceedingly short period of time. This means that if you plan on making money on the short term markets then you are going to need to be able to react quickly as well. The best way to react to profitable movement is to wait for the currency to reach a point where it is profitable before moving the stop to a point that is slightly in the money.

Chapter 6:
Tips for Success

Keep the risk in mind

Before you go ahead and make the decision to ultimately pull the trigger on any potential currency trade you are currently considering, the first thing you are going to want to go ahead and make sure that you know how likely you are to get your money back as well as actually turn a profit. This is why it is always so important to analyze the data that you gather as there is no other way of determining the mood the market is in which means essentially going into a trade just to gamble, and there are better ways to gamble than through the forex market. Additionally, you will want to know when to go ahead and cut your losses and having a clear idea of the overall level of risk will make this easier to determine as well.

With a clear idea of what sort of risk is going to be required for the trade in question, you will then have more tools at your disposal when it comes time to actually mitigate the risk that you have found, or at least to decrease it as much as possible.  Ensuring that the odds of actually turning a profit are in your favor means setting a tight stop loss and not letting your emotions get in the way in the heat of the moment. The point that you start a trade and the point that you set your stop loss at can be considered the maximum amount of risk you are accepting for a given trade.

It is important to always determine the acceptable amount of risk you can handle before you actually make the trade, when your emotions are of a nominal concern. If you wait to set a stop loss until after the trade is already in progress, then you run the risk of letting your emotions cloud your better judgement and losing profits in the process. If you feel the need to change your stop loss coming on then you are going to want to take a moment and consider exactly what it is you are thinking about doing and if it is something that you would consider if you were just getting in at that moment. With a few moment's consideration, your answer should be clear.

To keep your emotions from getting the better of you, prior to going into each trade you are going to want to keep in mind the point that you will always get out when you are happy with your profits, no matter what. When it comes to maximizing your profits, a stopping point is just as important as a good stop loss point. You may be tempted to stay in as long as possible in an effort to squeeze the most profit out of a good trade as possible, but this will lose you more than it will make you in the long run, guaranteed. Instead, the right choice is to cash out half of your holdings and then pick a new point further up so that you protect your profits while also maximizing them.

Finally, regardless of how much of a sure thing a specific trade may appear to be, you need to get in the habit of never investing more than you can afford to lose in a single trade. This means that if you start with $5,000 that you can invest in the forex market then you never want any single trade to cost you more than $100. This is what is known as the 2 percent rule and it is crucial to remaining financially solvent while investing in forex, especially when you are just starting out. While you will likely come up against moments where you want nothing more than to buck this trend, especially when you are riding high on a quality pair, sticking with it is what separates successful forex traders from amateurs. If you can't afford to lose it, don't put it in the pot, it is as simple as that.

Trade with the right mindset

If you ever hope to stick around the market long enough to think of yourself as an expert trader, there are several skills you are going to need to become very adept at using. First and foremost, this means always trading with a cool head, no matter what. When you are trading, your goal should be to be as emotionless and robotic as possible. The only thing that matters when you are trading is the numbers and if you worry about anything else while doing so, you are doing it wrong. Trading in the forex market successfully often means having the ability to make split second decisions, something that just can't be done if you let your emotions get in the way.

Understanding the fact that your emotions are only getting in the way and acting on that fact are two extremely different things. The first emotion that you are going to need to focus on banishing is anger. It can be easy to get angry when a trade that appears as though it is going to be a sure thing suddenly turns sideways, but a more effective use of that time is to instead immediately do what is required to minimize the losses, rather than standing there yelling at them. Aside from anger, the most common emotion that you are likely to come across is going to be fear. It can be easy to become afraid, especially if you broke the 2 percent rule and invested too heavily in a single pair; that doesn't mean it is productive, however, and indeed it can be even more dangerous than anger as it can be paralyzing as well. To prevent this from happening you will need to train yourself to push the emotion aside and act on the facts if you ever hope to find real success in the forex market.

Conclusion

Thank for making it through to the end of *FOREX: Definitive Beginner's Guide,* let's hope it was informative and able to provide you with all of the tools you need to achieve your goals both in the near term and for the months and years ahead. Remember, just because you've finished this book doesn't mean there is nothing left to learn on the topic. Becoming an expert at something is a marathon, not a sprint, slow and steady wins the race.

The next step is going to be to stop reading and to start preparing yourself to trade in the forex market successfully. When you are getting ready to get started you are going to want to do what you can to ensure that you keep your emotions in check at all times while also doing what you can to keep your expectations in check in terms of your early success rates. Additionally, it is important to consider the fact that the most reliable profits will come not from risky choices but from dedicated research and excellent timing.

Finally, if you found this book useful in anyway, a review on Amazon is always appreciated!

www.ingramcontent.com/pod-product-compliance
Lightning Source LLC
Chambersburg PA
CBHW071830200526
45169CB00018B/1303